My Heart on Your Sleeve

Samantha Turner

Copyright © 2019 Samantha Turner

This edition 2023

All rights reserved, including the right to reproduce this book, or portions thereof in any form. No part of this text may be reproduced, transmitted, downloaded, decompiled, reverse engineered, or stored, in any form or introduced into any information storage and retrieval system, in any form or by any means, whether electronic or mechanical without the express written permission of the author.

The views expressed in this work are solely those of the author and do not necessarily reflect the views of the publisher, and the publisher hereby disclaims any responsibility for them.

ISBN: 978-1-915889-47-8

PublishNation
www.publishnation.co.uk

A selection of heart felt, confused,

rambling and often dark poetry.

With thanks to my ever-patient mother Elaine,

my inspirational friend Chrissy,

and my loving husband Darren

for believing in me.

First Love

I remember loving as I had never loved before
Feeling as I had never felt
For with one kiss my soul would warm
And my heart would gladly melt
From a teenage dream you soon awaken
Joy turns into sorrow
Today you cry a waterfall
But the sun will rise again tomorrow

Nonsense

The wind took my hat
And my hair stuck to my lip-gloss
My hat flew down the road
Soon to be lost
I didn't chase it
Even though my ears were cold

Goodbye

I want to thank you for all the good times
And I forgive you for all the bad
Please cherish all of our memories
And the closeness we once had
I can't accept it's over
That our chapter has reached its end
Just let me sit here dreaming
Close my eyes so I can pretend
I realise now it's time
I'll give in and say goodbye
It's harder than I imagined
I promised not to cry
I wonder if you'll think of me
Maybe every now and then
Or will you be a stranger
Who used to be my friend

First Encounter

A familiar stranger, many weeks they had passed.
Again the looks. The eyes told of a great want and need on both sides.
A chemistry between two bodies living
in hope of a night soon to come.
Could hold back no longer
Words were spoken through cause of a friend.
Happiness but uncertainty. A chance was taken.
Relief and joy on both parts,
excitement and fear entwined.
Conversation and kisses, laughter and
light, mystery and fear of losing a just
found treasure.
More happiness. Smiles and affection, attraction,
distraction and proud to be seen together.
Arrangements, doubts, courage, sick reassurance and a
mind, body and soul living in hope. Maybe two.

Terror

I am the dark side of your soul
I am the demon without a face
I chase you in your nightmares
I am always there
Watching, waiting to take you to my world
My voice is the thunder
My face is fear
My touch is the chill down your spine
Feel me, fear me, hate me
For remember I am behind you
Always
Breathing in the dark

Betrayal

I'm hurting so much
I feel like I'm dying
And night after night
I sit here crying
I hate you for leaving
For going to her
But I'll walk around smiling
Pretend I don't care
Still inside there is pain
My heart is in two
I feel I have nothing
If I don't have you
I wonder if you think of me
While you're lying in her arms
It makes me feel like screaming
Yet surprisingly I'm calm
In time I'll come to realise
There's more to life than you
These bad times will make me stronger
Somehow I'll make it through
It's too hard to face the memories yet
I'll wait until I feel
A little bit less fragile
When the pain doesn't seem as real
You want the best of both worlds
But I won't be your bit on the side

Yes I may still love you
But I also have my pride

Vow

Be my angel
Be my guide
Be my comfort
When I try to hide
Be there when I need you
To wipe away my tears
Listen to my worries
Help me face my fears
Show me love and affection
Protection and care
Please never hurt me
Say you'll always be there

Missing You

I've never felt a want like this
A need so strong inside
I've lost count of all the sleepless nights
Of all the times I've cried
Everything about you
Your smile, your touch, your kiss
How you held my hand and pulled me close
All you did I miss
Now you're gone I have no sun
Only artificial light
Inside I face the darkness
Of lonely, eternal night

Continue

When it seems your world is empty
And inside you're full of pain
When all you feel is anger
And you need someone to blame
Sit back and take a breather
All isn't as it seems
Change is always around the corner
So don't ever lose your dreams
Lift your spirit high now
Leave the hurt you feel below
Make a new beginning
Go where you want to go
Take in everything around you
There's so much life still yet to live
All the world to visit
And so much love still yet to give
I know that life can hurt you
But don't let it wear you in
Remember, nothing lasts forever
If you try then you can win

Love Hurts

Love. It's like a little brother or sister, an endless torment
but you wouldn't live without it
It's the sun, it's the moon, it's the stars in the sky
It's the trees and the mountains
It's the birds that fly
Love. First comes the lust, the want, then
the need
A passion inside you growing like a seed
Second is devotion, the happiness and joy
You can't let go, like a child with a toy
Then comes the emptiness, the hurt and the fear
The pain inside, let out in a tear

Men

Men make you sad
They cause you pain
Men make you mad
They drive you insane
The things they promise
That look in their eyes
Your broken heart
Torn in two by their lies
But still we forgive
We give our heart back to them
They take it and smile
Then break it again

Unbearable Love

What would I do
If I never saw your face?
Never heard your voice
Or felt your warm embrace?
Time would have no meaning
Outside the world could end
For in my empty playpen
There would only be pretend
A single day without you
Feels much more like a year
My heart keeps being beaten
By hurt and pain and fear
I'm craving now to hold you
To never let you go
I think it's love I'm feeling
But I'll never let you know

Love Unrequited

One-sided love is worse than no love at all. You have so much to give and long to receive, trying desperately to fill the hollow deep inside but are given nothing but empty pleasure.

Longing for someone to take you in their loving arms, for them to hold you so tight.

There is only so hard you can try.

There comes a time when you must walk away.

Somewhere out there is the right person for you and they are looking for you right now. You'll know when they find you. You'll just know.

Damaged

I'm a little bit used
And slightly damaged
But over the years
I've somehow managed
To patch up my heart
And reset my mind
To give my secrets
To the darkness inside

There are cracks in the wall
But I've built it high
And the mistakes of youth
Have made me wise
I'm older and stronger
With life still to live
No more regrets
It's time to forgive

Shame

He made her no promises
He told her few lies
Yet still the flame of hope
Burned bright in her eyes
Why could he not love her
She was worthy, wasn't she?
For she asked him for nothing
But gave her love for free
For how much longer
Could her fragile heart cope?
As on another Mr wrong
She had pinned her dreams and hope
In her pretty eyes the flame has died
Extinguished by her tears
For she was nothing now, she knew inside
The truth, painfully clear
She went off the rails
No care for her soul
She punished herself
For she was worthless after all

Trapped

The mighty gales blow furious and free
Not caged by time and work and debt
As this working class existence has me
Tight by the throat, suffocating and kept

Trippy

Life is sliding away
Down the slope of time
Now I've no chance to play
Is it the beginning, or the start of the end?
I can't decide so I think I'll pretend
The sun is out
Shining on my skin
Should I open the door
And let the warmth come in?
I've got a lot of things
That I'd like to say
But my bottles broke
So I've thrown it away

No Way Out

No time to be free
While we are young
We are chained to the job
Without the job
We could not afford freedom
But the job costs us our time
So it is we have to work for fifty years so that we can
afford to be free once we are too old to truly feel alive

Ignorance

These thoughts like a whirlwind
Full of the debris the journey of my mind collects
A sponge soaking up new knowledge
Then the slow drip, drip of ignorance
As I begin to forget
An overwhelming nagging need to learn
Thoughts and ideas in my mind they burn
A raging flame to a tiny spark
It's flickered, it's died
And I'm worthless in the dark

Dark Secrets

The twisted tree
All gnarled and knotted
In the shadows of the forest
The world forgot it
The tree is old
The tree is wise
It remembers what it saw
With invisible eyes
Muffled screams
Dragging feet
The digging of earth
Dark and deep
Silently weeping
Unable to speak
This dark secret
The tree must keep
The birds don't utter it
In their evening song
Too sad to linger
The animals move on
The twisted tree
All knotted and gnarled
The forever keeper
Of the sleeping child

Enough

Leave me alone
To walk beneath the storm
That follows me around
There is no sun to rise at dawn
Only darkness fills my life
Bringing tears that fall as rain
Longing for the sunshine
To melt away my pain
I sleep within the shadows
In this world of fear and lies
Emptiness is my ruler
Any love I had has died

Again

At first they met as distant friends,
But time made them close.
Two bodies,
One mind with the same thought.
Soon their problems and secrets were shared
Touch of body and hands had hidden meaning afraid to be found. He wasn't free and he knew her view so, he tried to change things. A voice in her ear pulled her close, whispered what she wanted to hear. The words tripped out, the heart felt what the words meant. There was distance but closeness and strong determination. She knew what she wanted. Soon there was togetherness, heat and humour and happiness but it ended too soon. Two people. Life was against them. There was emptiness and fear and a heavy heart. Lies and unhappiness, one mind filled with confusion. What now? Why? And the sickening feeling of again.

True Love At Last

I was ice, cold and cruel
But you melted me
To fluid calmness in a pool
Of your love
A love that is timeless
Never-ending like space
And though our bodies may decay
Even death cannot erase
Your love
For you were born to save me from myself
And I was born to save you from yourself
Whatever has passed before
Does not matter anymore
Now we begin

Take Me There

Take me to the meadow
Where the colours dance and sway
I want to lie among the flowers
Watch the insects buzz and play

Take me to the river
Where the diamonds catch the light
I want to paddle in the splendour
Of the glistening water bright

Take me to the mountains
Where the mighty Eagles fly
I want to be atop the giants
Who lift me up to touch the sky

Take me to our home
that smells of coffee, cats and you
To sleep in our own bed my love
And dream of days anew

Raw

I tell myself we're over
So determined, so strong
Then I picture all the memories
And wonder what went wrong
They say that time will heal
That the pain will fade away
But sitting here in floods of tears
It doesn't feel that way
I pray to God to make things right
Better than they used to be
Silence is my only answer
I don't think he can hear me
Outside my life seems empty
There's no love to keep me warm
I long to just feel wanted
Now all I feel is torn
I need to breathe in deep
And lift my head up high
Ignore the heavy pain within
Forget I want to cry
If this is love I'd sooner hate
Hating is so much easier

Escape

Sit in silence
Live in pain
Filled full of hate
With no one to blame
That something inside you
Is eating you away
You just don't feel strong enough
To face another day
It is so easy to give in
To make the hurt just disappear
Take the only way out
Suddenly everything is clear
As you slowly slip away now
You finally feel release
Leave the painful world below you
Now the torture does then cease

Rich

We don't have much to call our own
No call to brag or boast
No money pots or fancy car
Yet we are better off than most

For I have you and you have me
A love that's strong and true
We live a happy, humble life
I'm rich in love with you

Anyone and No One

The old cannot stay
But youth is not guaranteed

Daydream

Find joy in every moment
See the blue behind the gray
Don't be ruled by fear and torment
But see the beautiful array
Of colours that dance
Alive in the light
Creating a story of rainbows
Against the shadows of the night
In times of loss and sorrow
In every drop of pain
Is a memory reflected
But the past cannot remain
There is no time to borrow
Our candle wick must burn
And soon we will be dust
Then to the stars we shall return

Not Just a Stranger

A familiar stranger, you entered my world, we spoke, we hugged on friendly terms. I wanted more, we thought alike but we were two separate minds as you held me tight.
Unsure by fear of pulling away, you took a chance, I wanted to stay. The flutter of excitement, the feel of your hands, your gentle voice, my fear of strange lands.
Disappointment, maybe lust in your eyes
I was being myself, I could only try. You did seem to want me, your voice remained soft, but I still can't help thinking you're another I've lost

Mental

You have a mental illness, He said
Me, Myself, not right in the head
I'm just a bit tired, stressed I'll be fine
No, you won't. You need therapy and time

I sit and cry, the confusion the shame
I'm a diagnosed basket case
There's something wrong with my brain

Overthinking, paranoid and scared
People are talking
They all think I'm weird

Let me just hide. Don't look at me, Don't speak
I can't face what I am
Not normal, a freak

A stranger in the mirror
I don't know who I am
Confident, happy girl
Come back if you can

Love Forever

Don't you dare leave me
We had a deal, you told me so
I was to go first
Don't pretend you didn't know

I thought we had forever
But time has tricked us all
Too busy making memories
Didn't know when we would fall

You gave me everything my love
I want another fifty years
I commit your touch to memory
As you wipe away my tears

This is not goodbye
It's "See you in a while"
Just wait for me my darling
I won't be far behind

Don't tell me life goes on
It ends with your last breath
Where you go I'll follow
Love forever, after death

Restless

I think my brain has a mind of it's own
It put songs in my head at night
When I want to go to sleep
Words come from my mouth
That I didn't even speak

The Quiet

Autumnal vale in the valley creeps
Across the water still
Ghostly giants behind do sleep
Their breath creates a chill
Most of life is hidden below
In earth so dark and warm
Waiting for the world to turn
And the land to be re born

More

Do not look back in regret, only forward in hope.
This is not the end.

About the Author

I live in the small Northern town of Wigan with my husband Darren. I enjoy walking in the countryside and caring for animals. I take inspiration for my writing from past and present experiences.

www.ingramcontent.com/pod-product-compliance
Lightning Source LLC
Chambersburg PA
CBHW070341120526
44590CB00017B/2971